Peace Be With You

Christ-Centered Bullying Solution

STUDENT WORKBOOK

by Frank A. DiLallo

Alliance for Catholic Education Press
at The University of Notre Dame

Notre Dame, Indiana

Copyright © 2011

Alliance for Catholic Education Press
University of Notre Dame
107 Carole Sandner Hall
Notre Dame IN 46556
http://acepress.nd.edu

ISBN: 978-1-935788-03-4

Interior layout: Julie Wernick Dallavis
Interior images: Shelley Kornatz

This book was printed on acid-free paper.

Printed in the United States of America.

My Name is_____

Welcome to the *Peace Be With You* Program!

Dear Student,

This is your personal workbook. It's filled with quotes, prayers, stories, activities, worksheets, and more. There is plenty of space for creative reflection, journaling, drawing, writing, and sharing with your classmates.

Share what's in this book and what you're learning with your parents, too!

There will be times when your teacher or another adult leader will ask you to complete worksheets and other activities in this book. This will help you follow along and have fun with all of the lessons in the program.

What you put into this program and book you will get out of this program and book!

Allow yourself to jump in with both feet. By doing so you will help make your class and your school an awesome place to learn and grow!

What's In This Book?

This program and workbook are divided into three phases:

Phase I: Christ Is Our Model for Leadership (pp. 3-34)

This phase supports you in exploring what it means to be a leader. Believe it or not, you have a lot of influence in your school. Everything you say or don't say, do or don't do, makes a difference! You are very important and play a big role in making your class and your school an awesome and cool place to learn and grow!

KEYWORDS LEADERSHIP • INSPIRATION • HONESTY • INTEGRITY • INFLUENCE
ATTITUDE • PASSION • ROLE MODEL • CHRIST-LIKE

Phase II: Dignity for All (pp. 35-52)

This phase will give you some helpful communication skills and a chance to practice using them. Good communication helps us clearly share our thoughts and ideas. Good communication can also be used to work out challenging situations with others in an effort to bring out the best in everyone. This phase does not expect students to all be close friends, but does invite everyone to at least be friendly with each other. How we treat others is how they will treat us in return.

KEYWORDS SAFETY • TRUST • PEER RELATIONSHIPS • COMMUNITY • EMPATHY
TEAMWORK • COMPASSION • COMMUNICATION
RECONCILIATION AND FORGIVENESS

Phase III: Pure of Heart (pp. 53-89)

This phase is a chance to deepen our relationship with our Lord and Savior Jesus Christ. Compassion and empathy for others comes from a Christ-centered place of inner peace and compassion. By daily practicing a prayerful and meditative state, we will make a big difference in how we treat our self and others. In this phase you will learn some helpful ways to deepen your prayer life, manage your stress, and other simple ways to take care of yourself. These helpful tips could even help you with your academic and extracurricular activities.

KEYWORDS PEACE • UNDERSTANDING • PRAYER • MEDITATION • KINDNESS
WHOLENESS • SPIRITUALITY • VISION • AFFIRMATION • SELF-CARE
STRESS • STRESS MANAGEMENT

PHASE I

Christ Is Our Model for Leadership

Prayer of
Blessed John XXIII

Lord Jesus Christ,
Who are called Prince of Peace.
Who are yourself our peace and reconciliation,
Who so often said, "Peace to you,"
Grant us peace.

Make all men and women witnesses of truth, justice, and
    brotherly love.
Banish from their hearts whatever might endanger peace.
Enlighten our rulers that they may guarantee and defend the
    great gift of peace.
May all peoples of the earth become as brothers and sisters.
May longed-for peace blossom forth and reign over us all.
Amen.

Christ Is Our Model for Leadership

Positive Leader Quotes

"A leader leads by example,
whether he intends to or not."

OSCAR WILDE

"A great leader's courage to fulfill his
vision comes from passion, not position."

JOHN MAXWELL

"Leadership is action, not position."

DONALD H. MCGANNON

Who Me? A Leader?

Reflect and journal what you learned from the first lesson on leadership.

_____

_____

_____

_____

_____

_____

_____

_____

_____

_____

_____

_____

_____

_____

_____

_____

_____

_____

_____

_____

_____

_____

Student Leader Folder

Use a two-pocket folder to hold a collection of items
that inspire you about leadership.

What to place in your Leader Folder:

- The list of leader words your class brainstormed together.

- Add new leader words to this list when you discover them.

- Journal about the leader words that best represent you and why.

- Journal about one leader word from the Leader Word List that you would like to develop more fully in yourself and why.

- Journal your own reflections about positive leadership.

- Journal concerns you have about current political or spiritual leaders. What would you do differently if you were in their position?

- Collect and add inspiring articles from magazines, newspapers, or Internet sources about leadership.

- Find and add quotes about positive leadership.

- Journal about your own personal leadership journey.

- Add anything else on leadership to your folder that you find interesting.

Whom Do I Admire?

Think of a person, real or fictitious, that you admire.
Reflect and write on the following questions:

Who is the person you chose? (Pick someone other than a parent)

_____

What positive characteristics, traits, or qualities do you admire in this person?

_____

_____

_____

What does or did this person do that is so admirable?

_____

_____

_____

What are some specific ways you strive to be more like this person?

_____

_____

_____

If possible ask this person if you can interview him or her. Use Worksheet 4 on p. 11 as a guide for the interview.

Tough Decisions

Scenario: A popular student has been bullying others by threatening to hurt them if they don't do what he or she wants them to do. You like this person but know what he or she is doing isn't respectful. Write your responses to the following questions:

What would your life be like if you followed this person?

_____

_____

_____

_____

What would your life be like if you stood up to this person and let him or her know what he or she is doing is wrong?

_____

_____

_____

_____

Describe how you would feel about yourself when you did the right thing.

_____

_____

_____

_____

List three people you could ask for help if you needed it:

1.

2.

3.

Parent Interview

Interview one of your parents or another relative.
Ask the following questions and record the responses:

Whom do you credit for influencing choices you have made in your life? Why?

_____

_____

_____

What did this person say or do that influenced your thinking and choices?

_____

_____

_____

What words of wisdom did he or she pass on that stick with you even today?

_____

_____

_____

What characteristics, traits, or qualities do you admire in this person?

_____

_____

_____

Which of these qualities do you believe you acquired from this person? How do you use these qualities to inspire others?

_____

_____

Positive Leader Interview

Thank you for your time today! What does it mean to be a positive leader?

_____

_____

_____

What important qualities make a great leader?

_____

_____

_____

Which of the qualities do you see in yourself?

_____

_____

_____

How do you think a person becomes a leader?

_____

_____

_____

Will you spend a few minutes a month mentoring me and helping me grow into a great leader? If not monthly, how often will work for you?

What would be a good day and time for you? What week is good in the month?

Circle One: **Monday**   **Tuesday**   **Wednesday**   **Thursday**   **Friday**

Time: Week   **1**   **2**   **3**   **4**

Thank you for the opportunity to meet with you about leadership today!
(_Make sure you extend a firm handshake!_)

Leader Reflection

Write a thoughtful reflection for a morning announcement
using what you learned from your interviews.

_____

_____

_____

_____

_____

_____

_____

_____

_____

_____

_____

_____

_____

_____

_____

_____

_____

Share your reflection with your teacher or principal!

Positive Leader Quotes

*"Change your thoughts
and you will change the world."*

NORMAN VINCENT PEALE

*"Leadership is practice
not so much in words
as in attitude and in actions."*

HAROLD GENEEN

*"The quality of a leader is reflected
in the standards they set for themselves."*

RAY KROC

Choose Your Flavor

Journal about how our attitude influences other people.

_____

_____

_____

_____

_____

Journal about how you influence others with your attitude.

_____

_____

_____

_____

_____

List three ways to change a negative attitude into a positive one:

    1.

    2.

    3.

List three ways you will be a "positive pebble in the school pond":

    1.

    2.

    3.

Choose Your Flavor

Write about a time when you were put down.

_____

_____

_____

How do you feel about being treated this way?

_____

_____

_____

How did you handle the situation?

_____

_____

_____

How would you handle the put-down if you were faced with it today?

_____

_____

_____

What difference does it make with how we handle situations like this?

_____

_____

_____

List three positive things you can do to prevent being put down ever again:

1.

2.

3.

Choose Your Flavor

Write on the following:

A time when you put someone down.

_____

_____

_____

How did you feel after the put-down? After a short time? After a longer period of time?

_____

_____

_____

How do you feel about treating another person this way?

_____

_____

Why did you put this person down? Were you trying to make yourself feel better? Were you trying to make the other person feel bad? Did this work?

_____

_____

_____

Did you increase or decrease your self-esteem by handling the situation this way? Why?

_____

_____

How could you have gotten what you wanted from the other student without putting him or her down?

_____

_____

How would you handle this situation today?

_____

_____

Choose Your Flavor

ACTION STEP:

Put up (compliment) as many classmates as you can today.

How do you feel when you are giving put-ups?

_____

_____

_____

How do people respond when you put them up?

_____

_____

_____

How do you feel after you see or hear the other person's response to your put-up?

_____

_____

_____

What would your school be like if everyone only gave put-ups to each other?

_____

_____

_____

How can you promote put-ups in your school?

_____

_____

_____

Choose Your Flavor

ACTION STEP:

Put up (compliment) one of your parents or another adult today.

How did you feel when you gave an adult a put-up?

_____

_____

_____

How did he or she respond?

_____

_____

_____

How did you feel after you saw the adult's response to your put-up?

_____

_____

_____

Ask one of your parents or an adult to give you a put-up.

_____

_____

_____

How did you feel when you received a put-up?

_____

_____

_____

What would your family be like if you only gave each other put-ups?

_____

_____

_____

Choose Your Flavor

Describe what your school would be like with only positive ripples.

_____

_____

_____

_____

_____

What would your school look like if it was the most amazing school on the planet?

_____

_____

_____

_____

_____

How would everyone be treating each other?

_____

_____

_____

_____

_____

What would everyone be saying? What would everyone be doing?

_____

_____

_____

_____

_____

Bully to Leader Quotes

"I suppose leadership at one time meant muscles, but today it means getting along with people."

MOHANDAS GANDHI

"If we did all the things we were capable of doing, we would literally astound ourselves."

THOMAS EDISON

"The key to successful leadership is influence, not authority."

KENNETH BLANCHARD

Bully to Leader

Journal how your understanding of being a leader has changed since the first session.

_____

_____

_____

_____

_____

_____

_____

_____

_____

_____

_____

_____

_____

_____

_____

Three things I learned about myself as a leader:

1.

2.

3.

Bully to Leader Role Plays

Write about what you learned from one of the two role plays:
"What Goes Around Comes Around" or "Odd Girl Out"

Here are some hints to help you get started:
- The "Passive Bystanders" are the most likely to help stop the bullying triangle.
- Everyone is responsible for bullying.
- Exclusion is hurtful and is a way of saying that we are better than someone else.
- How we treat others affects not only others but ourselves, too.
- What is the "code of silence" and how does it make the bullying problem worse?
- Having the courage to speak up is hard, but is what it takes to make a safe and amazing school.
- No one is better than anyone else. We are all equal.
- Other things not listed here that you might have learned from the role plays.

_____

_____

_____

_____

_____

_____

_____

_____

_____

_____

_____

_____

_____

_____

Bully to Leader Role Plays

Write about the person you identified with most in the first or second role play.

What role do you identify with? Why?

_____

_____

_____

What did you learn about yourself being in this role in real life?

_____

_____

_____

Do you like being in this role in real life?

_____

_____

_____

What choices do you have to help yourself get out of this role?

_____

_____

_____

What choices will build your self-esteem?

_____

_____

_____

List three people who will support you in making good choices:

1.

2.

3.

Bully to Leader Skit

Write a skit about disrespect or bullying behavior
that ends with a positive outcome. Keep safety in mind!

List your characters here:

_____

_____

_____

Write your script here:

_____

_____

_____

_____

_____

_____

_____

_____

_____

_____

_____

_____

_____

Share your script with your teacher, who will most likely allow you to perform your
skit in front of the class if there is enough class time and if your skit has a meaningful
lesson to teach your classmates.

Accountability Quotes

"I confess to Almighty God, and to you my brothers and sisters, that I have sinned through my own fault in my thoughts and in my words, in what I have done, and what I have failed to do."

PENITENTIAL RITE WITHIN LITURGY

"Success on any major scale requires you to accept responsibility. In the final analysis, the one quality that all successful people have is the ability to take on responsibility."

MICHAEL KORDA

"All blame is a waste of time. No matter how much fault you find with another, and regardless of how much you blame him, it will not change you."

WAYNE DYER

Accountability

Write about what it means to be accountable for my behavior.

_____

_____

How will I hold myself accountable for my behavior?

_____

_____

_____

What specific things will I do to show I am accountable for my behavior? (*Hint*: Admit it when you have not treated a person with respect. Let the person know what respectful behaviors you will show in the future.)

_____

_____

_____

_____

How can I hold others accountable for their behavior? (*Hint*: Let others know when they have not treated you or someone else with respect. Tell them you expect them to show you or others respect in the future.)

_____

_____

_____

_____

List three people who will help you hold yourself or others accountable:

1.

2.

3.

Historic Event

Write about a time in history when a group of people did what was popular, but not what was right. *Examples*: the Holocaust, Apartheid, Genocide, etc. Describe what it would take to make a situation like this "right."

_____

_____

_____

_____

_____

_____

How does it feel as you write about an event in history that has had a negative ripple in the world?

_____

_____

_____

What are you doing to create a positive ripple in the world?

_____

_____

_____

List three people who will support you in making a positive ripple in the world:

1.

2.

3.

Positive Leader Quotes

"Many a man would rather you heard his story than granted his request."

PHILLIP STANHOPE

"If your actions inspire others to dream more, learn more, do more, and become more, you are a leader."

JOHN QUINCY ADAMS

"The real voyage of discovery consists not in seeking new landscapes but in having new eyes."

MARCEL PROUST

Howard Gray Story

Write your reaction to the "Howard Gray" story.

_____

_____

_____

_____

_____

_____

_____

How many years after seventh grade did the author write this story?

_____

_____

What might the author have been feeling when he wrote this story?

_____

_____

_____

How can you "right" a "wrong" against another person or group?

_____

_____

_____

_____

_____

_____

Visioning Your Future

Journal what you think your life will be like in 20 years
if you use positive leadership skills now.

_____

_____

_____

_____

_____

_____

_____

_____

_____

_____

_____

_____

_____

_____

_____

_____

_____

_____

Code of Silence Story

Write your reaction to the "Code of Silence" story.

_____

_____

_____

_____

_____

_____

_____

_____

Do you think Frankie (the bully) showed strength or weakness in this story? How about Eric? How about Tommy? Why?

_____

_____

_____

_____

_____

_____

_____

Who is responsible for bullying? Frankie? Eric? Tommy? Why?

_____

_____

Code of Silence Rewrite

Rewrite the "Code of Silence" story in a way that would make it a win/win and have a positive rippling effect in the school.

_____

_____

_____

_____

_____

_____

_____

_____

_____

_____

Write about what you would say to Frankie, Tommy, and Eric if you had a chance to meet with them.

_____

_____

_____

_____

_____

_____

_____

Your Story

Write your own poem or story about bullying
from the viewpoint of the bully, target, or bystander.

_____

_____

_____

_____

_____

_____

_____

_____

_____

_____

_____

_____

_____

_____

_____

_____

_____

_____

_____

Ask your teacher if you can read your poem or story to the class.

Four Agreements

1. I agree to not bully anyone (including adults).

2. I agree to include anyone who is left out.

3. I agree to help myself and others (including adults) get closer to a 10.

4. I agree to SPEAK UP with two adults—one at school and one at home—whenever I see anyone not being treated like a 10.

Student Signature _____ Date _____
Parent Signature _____ Date _____
Teacher Signature _____ Date _____
Principal Signature _____ Date _____

- Take this contract home.
- Read this contract over with a parent.
- Sign this contract with a parent.
- Show this signed contract to your teacher and principal to sign.

PHASE II

Dignity for All

Prayer of St. Francis of Assisi

Lord, make me an instrument of your peace;
    where there is hatred, let me sow love;
    where there is injury, pardon;
    where there is doubt, faith;
    where there is despair, hope;
    where there is darkness, light;
    where there is sadness, joy.

O divine Master,
    grant that I may not so much seek to be consoled as to console;
    to be understood, as to understand;
    to be loved, as to love;
    for it is in giving that we receive,
    it is in pardoning that we are pardoned,
    and it is in dying that we are born to Eternal Life.

Amen.

Dignity for All

Quotes

"To err is human, to forgive divine."

ALEXANDER POPE

"The most important single ingredient in the formula of success is knowing how to get along with people."

THEODORE ROOSEVELT

"The significant problems we face cannot be solved at the same level of thinking we were at when we created them."

ALBERT EINSTEIN

Positive Leader Words

Add new positive leader words here:

_____

_____

_____

_____

_____

_____

_____

_____

_____

_____

Take one of the positive leader words on your list and write three ways you will put this word into action:

1.

2.

3.

List three people who will support you with this action:

1.

2.

3.

Safety Check

The goal in the last session was
"To help myself and others get closer to a 10."

What was your first Safety Check number? _____ (0-10)

What was your second Safety Check number? _____ (0-10)

Did you help yourself and others get closer to a 10?   **Y**   **N**   (Circle One)

If you answered yes, what helpful things did you contribute toward accomplishing this goal?

_____

_____

_____

_____

_____

If you answered no, what didn't you do to help accomplish this goal? Why?

_____

_____

_____

_____

List three things you will do throughout the year to accomplish this goal:

1.

2.

3.

360° Safety Diagram

During the program we used the term "Safety Check."
The Safety Check used is a continuum
from 0 being the least safe to 10 being the safest.

---

0   1   2   3   4   5   6   7   8   9   10

LEAST SAFE   **SAFEST**

In the community circle, you picked a number that best represented you and how safe you feel with your class. This next activity is similar to the Safety Check line above, but involves a circle called the 360° Safety Diagram.

Follow the directions below.

Directions:

1. Color each of the four quadrants in the 360° Safety Diagram (on the next page) to a number that best represents you.

2. Use a different color for each quadrant (Physical, Mental/Emotional, Social, and Spiritual).

3. On separate paper, write down the number you chose for each of the four quadrants. Add and divide by 4 to get your Safety Check number.

   Example: If your Physical quadrant = 6, Mental/Emotional = 8, Social = 3 and Spiritual = 7, you would add 6 + 8 + 3 + 7 = 24, then you would divide 24 ÷ 4 = 6.

4. The Safety Check number in this example is 6.

360° Safety Diagram

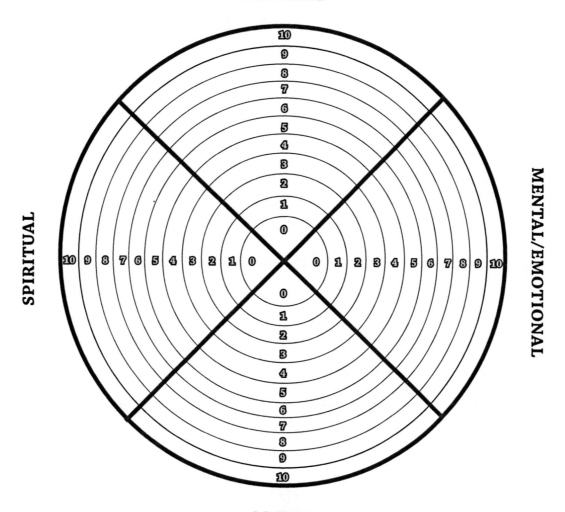

PHYSICAL

SPIRITUAL

MENTAL/EMOTIONAL

SOCIAL

PHYSICAL SAFETY	**SOCIAL SAFETY**
NO hitting, pushing, kicking, tripping, biting, choking, slapping, poking, hair pulling, pinching, nipple twisting = 10	NO relational aggression such as spreading rumors, ignoring, excluding, backbiting, cyber assaults = 10
MENTAL/EMOTIONAL SAFETY	**SPIRITUAL SAFETY**
NO put-downs about looks, hair, size or shape of body, wearing glasses or braces, how I walk or talk, grades (good or bad), name calling, clothes or shoes, color of my skin, whether I play sports or not = 10	NO put-downs around race, culture, religious preference, or religious practices. All race, religions and practices are supported and accepted = 10

Getting to 10

What or who is getting in the way of my being a 10? (10 = totally safe and thriving at my school)

_____

_____

_____

Whom do I need to do Clear Talk with to help me get closer to a 10?

_____

_____

How might my behavior get in the way of others being a 10?

_____

_____

_____

Whom do I need to do Clear Talk with so I can help them get closer to a 10?

_____

_____

_____

List three action steps you will take to make progress toward helping yourself and others get closer to a 10:

1.

2.

3.

Share this worksheet with your teacher or a parent.

Clear Talk

Step **1**   Thank you!

Step **2**   Data (What happened?)

Step **3**   Feelings: Mad, sad, glad, afraid, ashamed

Step **4**   My/Your behavior said....?

Step **5**   Wants

Use Clear Talk often to help build your communication skills and strengthen your relationships.

Peace Circle

Journal what you learned about yourself in the Peace Circle.

_____

_____

_____

_____

_____

_____

_____

_____

_____

_____

_____

_____

_____

_____

_____

_____

_____

_____

_____

Clear Talk Practice

Imagine Howard Gray did Clear Talk with author Lee Domann
while they were still in school. Using the five steps in Clear Talk,
write what you think Howard might say to Lee.

Step **1**   Thank you!

Step **2**   Data (What Happened?)

_____

_____

Step **3**   Feelings (Mad, Sad, Glad, Afraid, Ashamed)

_____

_____

Step **4**   Your behavior said.....?

_____

_____

Step **5**   Wants

_____

_____

Do you identify more with Howard or with Lee? Why?

_____

_____

_____

_____

_____

Clear Talk Practice

Imagine Frankie (bully) did Clear Talk with Tommy (target)
while they were still in school. Using the five steps in Clear Talk,
write what you think Frankie might say to Tommy.

Step **1** Thank you!

Step **2** Data (What Happened?)

_____

_____

Step **3** Feelings (Mad, Sad, Glad, Afraid, Ashamed)

_____

_____

Step **4** Your behavior said.....?

_____

_____

Step **5** Wants

_____

_____

Do you identify more with Frankie, Tommy, or Eric (active bystander)? Why?

_____

_____

_____

_____

_____

Clear Talk Practice

Write out a Clear Talk you want to do with a classmate.
Only follow through with this Clear Talk in a class meeting with
your teacher or school counselor present to support you.

Step **1**   Thank you!

Step **2**   Data (What Happened?)

_____

_____

Step **3**   Feelings (Mad, Sad, Glad, Afraid, Ashamed)

_____

_____

Step **4**   Your behavior said.....?

_____

_____

Step **5**   Wants

_____

_____

What is at risk if you follow through with this Clear Talk?

_____

_____

What is at risk if you don't follow through with this Clear Talk?

_____

_____

CLEAR Listening Quotes

"Be a good listener.
Your ears will never get you in trouble."

FRANK TYGER

"To say that a person feels listened to
means a lot more than just their ideas
get heard. It's a sign of respect.
It makes people feel valued."

DEBORAH TANNEN

"You cannot truly listen to anyone
and do anything else at the same time."

M. SCOTT PECK

CLEAR Listening

The listener plays an important role in Clear Talk, too!
Use the acronym "CLEAR" to help you keep in mind
some key tips about being a good listener.

 Connect face to face. This is an important part of building relationships. By connecting with others and using good communication, we become better people.

 Listen with your eyes, ears, and heart. A good listener is open, still, and does not disrupt or interrupt the speaker.

 Eye Contact is a great way to tune into what a person is saying.

 Attentive Focus on what the speaker is saying. Give them your full attention. Look interested!

 Respectful means being kind and considerate of what the person is saying. You don't have to agree or disagree, just listen. The letter R also stands for **Relaxed**. Stay as relaxed as you can and just hear the person out.

Trust and believe you have something to learn
by being a CLEAR listener!

CLEAR Listening Example

Step 1

Speaker: "**Thank you!**"
Listener: "Thank you for asking me to do Clear Talk with you."

Step 2

Data (What happened?)
Speaker: "A month ago you pushed me down on the playground. I skinned my hands, and you laughed at me."
Listener: "What I hear you saying is I pushed you down on the playground, you skinned your hands, and I laughed at you."

Step 3

Feelings (Mad, Sad, Glad, Afraid, Ashamed)
Speaker: "I feel mad at you for pushing me down, humiliated when you laughed at me, and afraid you'll do it again."
Listener: "I hear you're feeling mad, humiliated, and afraid."

Step 4

Your behavior said.....?
Speaker: "Your behavior said you disrespected me by pushing me down, your behavior hurt my hands, and I was humiliated me when you laughed at me."
Listener: "What I hear you saying is I disrespected you when I pushed you down, I hurt your hands, and I humiliated you when I laughed."

Step 5

Wants
Speaker: "I want you to promise you'll never do this again. I want you to apologize for what you did. I want you to put me up from now on."
Listener: "What I hear you saying is you want me to promise to never treat you this way again, you want me to apologize for what I did, and put you up from now on."

The listener can respond to the speaker following CLEAR Listening. When both speaker and listener are "complete," some sign of peace is exchanged.

CLEAR Listening

Journal about a time when you were a CLEAR Listener.

_____

_____

_____

_____

_____

What was the speaker's reaction to your CLEAR Listening?

_____

_____

Whom in your life do you go to for CLEAR Listening?

_____

_____

What are the gifts of being a CLEAR Listener?

_____

_____

_____

What are the gifts for us when we receive CLEAR Listening?

_____

_____

_____

_____

Clear Talk

Teach Clear Talk to one of your parents.
Use a real life situation to practice and help build your confidence.

Write out what you would say below. Use this to practice or during your actual Clear Talk with your parent.

Step 1   Thank you!

Step 2   Data (What Happened?)

_____

_____

Step 3   Feelings (Mad, Sad, Glad, Afraid, Ashamed)

_____

_____

Step 4   Your behavior said...?

_____

_____

Step 5   Wants

_____

_____

Teach one of your parents CLEAR Listening. Have he or she reflect on what you say.

1 "Thank you for asking me to do Clear Talk with you."
2 "What I heard you say the data is...."
3 "What I heard you say your feeling is...."
4 "My/Your behavior said...."
5 "What I heard you want is...."

PHASE III

Pure of Heart

Prayer of St. Teresa of Avila

Let nothing disturb you.
Let nothing frighten you.
All things are passing;
God never changes.
Patience gains all things.
Who has God wants nothing.
God alone suffices.

Pure of Heart

Pure of Heart Quotes

"Kindness is a language we all understand. Even the blind can see it and the deaf can hear it."

MOTHER TERESA

"While you are proclaiming peace with your lips, be careful to have it even more fully in your heart."

ST. FRANCIS OF ASSISI

"Your work is to discover your world and then with all your heart give yourself to it."

BUDDHA

Peace Circle 2

Journal what you learned from the Peace Circle about connecting with yourself, others, and God.

_____

_____

_____

_____

_____

_____

_____

_____

_____

_____

_____

_____

_____

_____

_____

_____

_____

_____

_____

Living in "Fast Forward"

*"There is more to life
than increasing its speed."*

MAHATMA GANDHI

*"For fast acting relief,
try slowing down."*

LILY TOMLIN

*"Some of the secret joys of living
are not found by rushing from point A
to point B, but by inventing some
imaginary letters along the way."*

DOUGLAS PAGELS

Living in "Fast Forward"

1. Write about a time when you hurried or rushed to get somewhere or do something.

_____

_____

_____

2. Who was with you? How were you treating each other?

_____

_____

_____

3. What was physically happening inside of you while you were hurrying?

_____

_____

_____

4. What were you thinking while you were rushing around?

_____

_____

_____

5. What were you feeling emotionally in this hurried state?

_____

_____

_____

6. What were the consequences of this hurried pace for you and everyone else?

_____

_____

_____

Continue this exercise on the next page.

Living in "Fast Forward"
(continued)

7. What does leading a balanced life mean to you?

_____

_____

_____

8. What is your life like when it gets out of balance?

_____

_____

_____

9. How do advertisements and commercials play on how we feel about ourselves?

_____

_____

_____

Pair up with a partner and share what you wrote with each other.

List what you have in common with your partner.

_____

_____

_____

_____

List your unique differences.

_____

_____

_____

_____

Share what you learned with the entire class.

Technology & Cyberbullying

What is helpful about technology?

_____

_____

_____

What are some ways technology can be hurtful? (*Hint*: cyberbullying)

_____

_____

_____

List five positive ways cyberbullying can be stopped among students:

1.

2.

3.

4.

5.

What positive actions can you take to stop cyberbullying?

_____

_____

_____

List three people you will team up with to end cyberbullying:

1.

2.

3.

Understanding Stress Quotes

*"Is everything as urgent
as your stress would imply?"*

CARRIE LATET

*"Stress is the trash of modern life.
We all generate it but if you don't
dispose of it properly, it will pile up
and overtake your life."*

DANZAE PACE

*"Stress is an ignorant state.
It believes everything is an emergency."*

NATALIE GOLDBERG

Understanding Stress

1. Write what the word "stress" means to you.

_____

_____

_____

2. How is stress beneficial?

_____

_____

_____

3. Where does stress show up in your body?

_____

_____

_____

4. Why do some people get headaches? What messages might headaches give us?

_____

_____

_____

5. What are some natural ways to relieve a headache instead of taking a drug?

_____

_____

_____

6. What does healthy eating and staying hydrated have to do with our mood, attitude, and overall health?

_____

_____

_____

Continue this exercise on the next page.

Understanding Stress

(continued)

7. What are some physical consequences of too much stress?

_____

_____

Mental or emotional consequences?

_____

_____

Social consequences?

_____

_____

Relational consequences?

_____

_____

Spiritual consequences?

_____

_____

Pair up with a partner and share what you wrote with each other.

What do you share in common with your partner?

_____

_____

_____

What are the unique differences between you and your partner?

_____

_____

_____

Share what you learned with the class.

Understanding Stress

1. Write about a time in your life when you felt a lot of stress. What happened that caused the stress?

_____

_____

2. How did you treat yourself and others when you were under stress?

_____

_____

3. What did you do to try to manage your stress? Did it help?

_____

_____

4. List three new healthy ways to reduce stress that you can add to your "Stress Less Tool Kit":

    1.

    2.

    3.

5. Why is coping with life situations in a healthy way so important?

_____

_____

Pair up with a partner and share what you wrote with each other.

What do you share in common with your partner?

_____

_____

What are the unique differences between you and your partner?

_____

_____

Share what you learned with the entire class.

Stress Less Theatre Production

In your small group choose **one** of the two options below.
You have 15 minutes to prepare. Follow your teacher's instructions
on what to do next.

Option One:

Create a skit, pantomime, or rap song that demonstrates what stress means to you.

Include the following:

- Ways stress can affect us in body, mind, and spirit
- Healthy ways we can manage our stress

Option Two:

Create a parody of what advertisements or commercials are "really saying."

Include the following:

- Ways advertisements and commercials can affect us in body, mind, and spirit
- Insightful ways to help us see the truth behind commercial messages

"The Gift" Quotes

*"Where there is no vision,
the people perish."*

PROVERBS 29:18

*"You weren't an accident.
You weren't mass-produced.
You aren't an assembly line product.
You were deliberately planned, specifically
gifted and lovingly positioned on the
Earth by the Master Craftsman."*

MAX LUCADO

*"Imagination is more important
than knowledge."*

ALBERT EINSTEIN

"The Gift"

1. Write about how you take care of yourself in body, mind, and spirit.

_____

_____

2. What are some ways you could take better care of yourself in these areas?

_____

_____

3. Why do alcohol, tobacco, or other drugs keep us from being the person we are meant to be?

_____

_____

4. List three people that will support you in staying drug free:

    1.

    2.

    3.

5. How does bullying behavior keep the Bully, Target, and Active or Passive Bystanders from being all they are meant to be?

_____

_____

Pair up with a partner and share what you wrote with each other.

6. What do you share in common with your partner?

_____

_____

7. What are the unique differences between you and your partner?

_____

_____

Share what you learned with the entire class.

My Ideal School

In your small group:
- Choose a *Facilitator* to ask your group the questions below.
- Choose a *Time Keeper* to keep time allowing for 1 minute per question.
- Choose a *Recorder* to write down the highlights of what is said during discussion.
- Choose a *Reporter* to report the group's answers to the class.

Discuss the following questions with your small group:

During the "ideal school" visual exercise:

1. What did you see happening at your ideal school?

_____

_____

2. How are you being treated?

_____

_____

3. How are you treating others?

_____

_____

4. How is everyone treating each other?

_____

_____

5. How important do you feel in your ideal school? Valued? Respected?

_____

_____

6. What is your Safety Check number at your ideal school?

_____

_____

Finding Christ

In your small group:

- Keep the same *Facilitator* to ask your group the questions below.
- Keep the same *Time Keeper* to make sure everybody gets 1 minute to share.
- The *Recorder* and *Reporter* can relax this round!

During the visual exercise:

1. What is your ideal school like now that Christ has filled your heart? (Look like? Feel like? Sound like?)

_____

_____

2. How do you see yourself treating others from a Christ-filled place?

_____

_____

3. Can your classmates sense the love God has for you?

_____

_____

4. Do you feel important, valued, respected by our loving God?

_____

_____

5. What is your Safety Check number right now?

_____

_____

6. What did Christ say to you about why you are here on this planet and what He is calling you to do?

_____

_____

7. What else happened that you would like to share?

_____

_____

Relaxation Quotes

*"The time to relax is when
you don't have time for it."*

SYDNEY J. HARRIS

*"By letting go it all gets done;
the world is won by those who let it go."*

THE TAO TE CHING

*"How beautiful it is to do nothing,
and then to rest afterward."*

SPANISH PROVERB

Relaxation Tip # 1

Stress Check

On the Stress Check continuum below, 0 represents the lowest stress level you have ever experienced and 10 is the highest.

Pick a number that best represents your stress level right now.

Write your Stress Check number here _____

STRESS CHECK

0 1 2 3 4 5 6 7 8 9 10

Low Stress   High Stress

Relaxation Tip # 2

Breath Check

List three things that happen in the body when you take shallow breaths because of stress:

1.

2.

3.

List three things you experience when you take slow deep breaths:

1.

2.

3.

"Smile, breathe, and go slowly."

THICH NHAT HANH

Relaxation Tip # 3

Tension Check

List where your tension spots are located when you are stressed out:

1.
_____

_____

2.
_____

_____

3.
_____

_____

4.
_____

_____

5.
_____

_____

Communicate with your tension spots reminding them to let go....to loosen the grip.

*"Tension is who you think you should be.
Relaxation is who you are."*

CHINESE PROVERB

Relaxation Tip # 4

Balance Check

- Stand tall with your feet shoulder width apart and toes pointing straight ahead.
- Place your arms and hands at your side. Feel the balance. This is base position.
- Lift one foot and then your entire leg to contrast balance and imbalance.
- Come back to base position.

List three things you will do to help yourself stay balanced:

1.

_____

_____

2.

_____

_____

3.

_____

_____

"Be aware of wonder. Live a balanced life—learn some and think some and draw and paint and sing and dance and play and work every day some."

ROBERT FULGHUM

Short Meditation

Journal your experience from the short meditation.

_____

_____

_____

_____

_____

_____

_____

_____

_____

_____

_____

_____

_____

_____

_____

_____

_____

_____

_____

Redoing Your Stress Check

Pick a number that best represents your current stress level.

Stress Check number before the meditation   _____

Stress Check number after the meditation   _____
(Subtract the top number from the bottom number)

Current Stress Check number   _____

Give yourself a pat on the back for taking the time to "Stress Less!"

STRESS CHECK

0 1 2 3 4 5 6 7 8 9 10

Low Stress   High Stress

PeaceScape Drawing

PeaceScape Sharing

Pair up with a partner.
Decide who will be the listener and who will be the speaker.
Switch when instructed to do so by your teacher.

Speaker: Show your PeaceScape to your partner.
Listener: Admire your partner's PeaceScape.
Speaker: Tell your partner about your PeaceScape. Share with your partner:

1. Why you used the colors you did in your PeaceScape?

2. What meaning do shapes or symbols hold in your PeaceScape?

3. If you drew human figures in your PeaceScape, who are they? Why did you put them in your PeaceScape?

4. During the meditation, who was surrounding you? Supporting you? Celebrating you?

5. How did they celebrate you?

6. What importance does a supportive circle of family and friends hold in your life?

7. Who supports you most in being the best person you can be?

8. How can you and your partner support each other?

9. Thank your partner for sharing.

10. Partners share what they learned with the class.

Put-Down Messages

Think about a time when you were put down.

Write down the put-down messages you heard about yourself from others.

_____

_____

_____

_____

_____

_____

_____

Write down all the put-down messages you say about yourself that are in your head. *Examples*: "I can't, I'm stupid, I'm not as good as...," etc.

_____

_____

_____

_____

_____

_____

_____

Take your list of "Put-Down Messages" and apply them
to the Shift Formula on the next page.

Shift Formula

Recognize the negative words or phrases you hear playing in your head.

Obliterate the unwanted messages using an "Obliterator Word" you will remember such as *Delete, Clear, Let go, Erase, Shake, Give up* or make up your own "Obliterator Word."

Replace the unwanted message choosing a "Welcoming Word" you will remember such as *Repeat, Hear, Know, Replace, Make, Receive* or make up your own "Welcoming Word."

Repeat the desired message over and over until you believe the message.

Here are some examples:

Obliterator Words		Shift to	Welcoming Words
Delete	*doubts*	Repeat	*"I am confident."*
Clear	*"I'm not good enough."*	Hear	*"I am good enough."*
Let go	*"I'm not lovable."*	Know	*"I am lovable."*
Erase	*"I can't do it."*	Replace	*"I can do it."*
Shake	*bad decisions*	Make	*good decisions*
Give up	*put-downs*	Receive	*put-ups*

Use the next page to fill in your "Obliterator" and "Welcoming Words."

Shift Formula

Recognize the negative words or phrases you hear playing in your head.

Obliterate the unwanted messages using an "Obliterator Word" you will remember such as *Delete, Clear, Let go, Erase, Shake, Give up* or make up your own "Obliterator Word."

Replace the unwanted message choosing a "Welcoming Word" you will remember such as *Repeat, Hear, Know, Replace, Make, Receive* or make up your own "Welcoming Word."

Repeat the desired message over and over until you believe the message.

Use the "Obliterator" and "Welcoming Word" that works for you:

Obliterator Words...........Shift to...........Welcoming Words			
Delete	_____	Repeat	_____
Clear	_____	Hear	_____
Let go	_____	Know	_____
Erase	_____	Replace	_____
Shake	_____	Make	_____
Give up	_____	Receive	_____

Use this formula often to change negative thoughts into positive thoughts!

Getting Rid of Put-Down Messages

Do something fun (but safe)
to get rid of your put-down messages.

Take the sheet with the put-down messages on it and:

- Make an airplane and fly it around the room and into the wastebasket.

- Rip up the paper and toss into the air and then pick up the pieces and toss them in the wastebasket.

- Wad up the paper and toss into the wastebasket.

- Put it in a shredder.

Affirmation Quotes

"Constant repetition carries conviction."

ROBERT COLLIER

"It's the repetition of affirmations that leads to belief. And once that belief becomes a deep conviction, things begin to happen."

CLAUDE M. BRISTOL

"Relentless, repetitive self talk is what changes our self-image."

DENIS WAITLEY

Crafting a Positive Affirmation

Follow these six guidelines for crafting a positive affirmation.

1. Write a positive affirmation. Keep it short and simple. Check out the examples on the next page if needed.

2. Use positive words of encouragement.

3. Write the affirmation in two ways, first using "I" and then using "you."

4. Include a positive emotion.

5. Phrase the affirmation as fact.

6. Say, write, or sing your affirmation frequently.

_____

_____

_____

_____

_____

_____

_____

_____

Positive Affirmation Examples

I am safe and at peace in my body.
You are safe and at peace in your body.

I am special and celebrate my uniqueness.
You are special and celebrate your uniqueness.

I am positive in my attitude.
You are positive in your attitude.

I am good enough.
You are good enough.

I am loved and accepted as I am.
You are loved and accepted as you are.

I am capable of being a great thinker.
You are capable of being a great thinker.

I am grateful for my life.
You are grateful for your life.

I am strong in my faith.
You are strong in your faith.

I am confident and capable of making good decisions.
You are confident and capable of making good decisions.

I accept the feelings I have in any given moment as my inner truth.
You accept the feelings you have in any given moment as your inner truth.

I speak up for myself.
You speak up for yourself.

I am surrounded by loving-kindness.
You are surrounded by loving-kindness.

I am treating problems as opportunities to grow in wisdom and love.
You are treating problems as opportunities to grow in wisdom and love.

I am worthy of all the good in my life.
You are worthy of all the good in your life.

I am imaginative and creative.
You are imaginative and creative.

I am confident my future is bright and promising.
You are confident your future is bright and promising.

I celebrate my accomplishments.
You celebrate your accomplishments.

I am patient and tolerant of differences in others.
You are patient and tolerant of differences in others.

I surround myself with people who support me in making healthy choices.
You surround yourself with people who support you in making healthy choices.

Strength Bombardment

List five things you heard your classmates say to put you up:

1.

2.

3.

4.

5.

How did this make you feel to hear these things from your classmates?

_____

_____

_____

How did it feel to give your classmates put-ups?

_____

_____

_____

When you heard these things did it move your Safety Check number closer to a 10? Why?

_____

_____

_____

List three things you will do to help keep put-ups going in your class and in your school.

1.

2.

3.

Buddy Up!

My buddy's name is: _____

Five things I learned about my Buddy Up! buddy are:

1.

2.

3.

4.

5.

Three things my Buddy Up! buddy learned about me are:

1.

2.

3.

Write about what you learned about yourself because you participated in Buddy Up!

_____

_____

_____

_____

_____

_____

_____

Long Meditation

Journal your experience from the Long Meditation.

_____

_____

_____

_____

_____

_____

_____

_____

_____

_____

_____

_____

_____

_____

_____

_____

_____

_____

_____

_____

An Irish Prayer

May God give you....
For every storm, a rainbow,
For every tear, a smile,
For every care, a promise,
And a blessing in each trial.
For every problem life sends,
A faithful friend to share,
For every sigh, a sweet song,
And an answer for each prayer.

An Irish Blessing

May the road rise up to meet you.
May the wind always be at your back.
May the sun shine warm upon your face.
And rains fall soft upon your fields.
And until we meet again,
May God hold you in the palm of His hand.

CPSIA information can be obtained at www.ICGtesting.com
Printed in the USA
LVOW09s0923010813

345527LV00002B/5/P